MACK MODEL B
1953-1966
PHOTO ARCHIVE

MACK MODEL B
1953-1966
PHOTO ARCHIVE

Photographs from the
Mack Trucks Historical Museum Archives

Edited with introduction by
Thomas E. Warth

Iconografix
Photo Archive Series

Iconografix
P.O. Box 18433
Minneapolis, Minnesota 55418 USA

Library of Congress Card Number 94-76264

ISBN 1-882256-19-0

94 95 96 97 98 99 00 5 4 3 2 1

Cover and book design by Lou Gordon, Osceola, Wisconsin

Printed in the United States of America

Book trade distributed by Voyageur Press, Inc. (800) 888-9653

PREFACE

The histories of machines and mechanical gadgets are contained in the books, journals, correspondence and personal papers stored in libraries and archives throughout the world. Written in tens of languages, covering thousands of subjects, the stories are recorded in millions of words.

Words are powerful. Yet, the impact of a single image, a photograph or an illustration, often relates more than dozens of pages of text. Fortunately, many of the libraries and archives that house the words also preserve the images.

In the *Photo Archive Series*, Iconografix reproduces photographs and illustrations selected from public and private collections. The images are chosen to tell a story—to capture the character of their subject. Reproduced as found, they are accompanied by the captions made available by the archive.

The Iconografix *Photo Archive Series* is dedicated to young and old alike, the enthusiast, the collector and anyone who, like us, is fascinated by "things" mechanical.

ACKNOWLEDGMENTS

The photographs and illustrations appearing in this book were made available by the Mack Trucks Historical Museum. We are grateful to Colin Chisholm, Curator, for his assistance.

B77ST diesel 6-wheel tractor at the Yonkers Exit, New York State Thruway. February 1959.

INTRODUCTION

"Built like a Mack Truck"— what a wonderful statement—one of the best descriptions you can give to a piece of equipment designed to stand up to tough conditions. Since just after the turn of the century, Mack has been turning out trucks of such a quality that the phrase has become part of our language. The first truck placed in the Smithsonian Collection was a Model AC—the venerable "Bulldog".

The Mack brothers first made their name as horse drawn wagon builders in Brooklyn, New York in the 1800s. Early buses were built in New York but it was in Allentown, Pennsylvania that the company became fully established. The years between the two World Wars saw numerous changes in corporate structure, yet during this time Mack became one of the world's foremost truck manufacturers. Like all industry, Mack was put under government control during World War II. Over 30,000 vehicles were built, and Mack components were installed in tanks and put to many other uses.

At the end of the war, the pent-up demand for trucks was mainly filled by resuming manufacture of pre-war models. Meanwhile, development commenced on new models using some of the design lessons of the war years. During this period, as the long-haul trucking industry developed, Mack was involved in much public relations work to negate attacks on the industry by the railroad lobby. At the same time, there was a reluctance in the industry to accept the diesel engine. During the B model years of 1953 to 1966 this attitude changed. By the 1960s, diesel was accepted for most heavy-duty applications.

The Model B became one of Mack's most successful models, with over 125,000 vehicles sold. It was revolutionary in appearance for its time. The rounded lines of its cab and hood were striking to look at, and the design also served the purpose of leaving more room for larger engines as they became available. The "contoured" cab of some tractors was an effort to increase trailer size without exceeding the 45 feet overall size limit in some areas. Cab design on some later units was modified, and some larger versions lost the appeal of the early fifties' designs.

Mack Model B 1953-1966 Photo Archive presents a cross section of photographs selected from the Mack Trucks Historical Museum. They are presented in roughly chassis capacity order and without editorial comment. Where possible, we have given the negative number as recorded in the archive. Captions are a literal interpretation of the information printed on the archive photograph. The first digit of the model number indicated approximate gross vehicle/combination weight: 4 indicated from 30,500 to 53,000 pounds; 6 from 30,500 to 76,800 pounds; 7 from 65,000 to 76,800 pounds; 8 from 51,000 to 100,000 pounds; even numbered second digits indicated models equipped with gasoline engines; odd numbered second digits indicated models equipped with diesel engines. A complete list of B Series model numbers, build dates, and production figures appear in an appendix. We hope that by presenting these fascinating images the reader will be encouraged into further research.

Mack Plant Number 4 in Allentown where most of the Model Bs were built. (AK92925-2)

B Series assembly line at Allentown.

B Series assembly line at Allentown.

Cover illustration from 1953 Mack Trucks
Annual Report.

B30P gasoline 4-wheel platform truck. July 1957. (M16938)

B30P gasoline 4-wheel platform truck. January 1955. (M16368)

B30P gasoline 4-wheel platform truck. March 1958. (M17068)

B30X gasoline 4-wheel heavy duty truck. April 1953. (C7271)

B30X gasoline 4-wheel heavy duty truck. September 1953. (M15976)

B30S gasoline 6-wheel truck. September 1953. (C7546)

B30T gasoline 4-wheel tractor. April 1955. (M16427)

B30T gasoline 4-wheel tractor. July 1954. (C7781)

B33S diesel 6-wheel truck. (399)

B332P diesel 4-wheel platform truck, front-wheel-drive. February 1963. (E7060)

EN401 401 cubic inch gasoline engine as used in B42s. December 1957. (C11119)

B42P gasoline 4-wheel platform truck. April 1953. (C7211)

B42P gasoline 4-wheel platform truck. August 1954. (M16267)

B42P gasoline 4-wheel platform truck. October 1954. (M16327)

B42S gasoline 6-wheel truck. (375)

B42S gasoline 6-wheel truck. (M16037)

B42S gasoline 6-wheel trucks. January 1955. (M16379)

B42S gasoline 6-wheel truck. February 1955. (M16493)

B42S gasoline 6-wheel truck.

B42S gasoline 6-wheel truck.

B42S gasoline 6-wheel truck.

B43S diesel 6-wheel trucks.

B421S gasoline 6-wheel truck. August 1955. (C9015)

B426S gasoline 6-wheel truck, front-wheel-drive. April 1958. (C11244)

40

B426S gasoline 6-wheel truck, front-wheel-drive. May 1958. (C11289)

B426S gasoline 6-wheel truck, front-wheel-drive, heavy duty. (360)

B4226SX gasoline 6-wheel truck, front-wheel-drive, heavy duty. April 1961. (C12176)

B42T gasoline 4-wheel tractor. February 1953. (C7130)

B42T gasoline 4-wheel tractor. February 1953. (C7123)

B42T gasoline 4-wheel tractor. April 1955. (M16424)

Mack models B42, B42, LFT, EH, B42T, and D--all with tanker bodies.

B42T gasoline 4-wheel tractor. November 1954. (C8248)

B42T gasoline 4-wheel tractor. November 1954. (C8253)

B421T gasoline 4-wheel tractor. December 1954. (C8322)

B42T gasoline 4-wheel tractors.

B42T gasoline 4-wheel tractor. September 1958. (M17129)

B42T gasoline 4-wheel tractor. (I1596)

B42TPB gasoline 4-wheel piggy-back tractor. June 1958. (E2416)

B43T diesel 4-wheel tractor.

B42TPB gasoline 4-wheel piggy-back tractor. May 1959. (E2371)

B42ST gasoline 6-wheel tractor. May 1953. (C7347)

B43ST diesel 6-wheel tractor. February 1958. (M17051)

B44TPB gasoline 4-wheel piggy-back tractor. July 1956. (C9809)

B47X diesel 4-wheel and B47S diesel 6-wheel heavy duty trucks. (1199)

B47T diesel 4-wheel tractors. (1201)

B46S gasoline 6-wheel truck. June 1958. (C11319)

B462SX gasoline 6-wheel truck, front-wheel-drive, heavy duty. 1960. (M17418)

B50T gasoline 4-wheel tractor. (C7281)

B50T gasoline 4-wheel tractor. May 1953. (C7321)

B50T gasoline 4-wheel tractor. November 1953. (M16060)

66

B53S diesel 6-wheel truck.

B53S diesel 6-wheel truck. May 1963. (C12587)

B53S diesel 6-wheel truck. May 1963. (C12590)

B57S diesel 6-wheel truck, heavy duty. June 1964. (C12765)

B576S diesel 6-wheel truck, front-wheel-drive, heavy duty. March 1965. (C12824)

B576S diesel 6-wheel truck, front-wheel-drive, heavy duty. March 1965. (C12823)

B576S diesel 6-wheel truck, front-wheel-drive, heavy duty. March 1965. (C12829)

END673 672 cu in diesel engine as used in B61 models. June 1957. (C10791)

B61X diesel 4-wheel truck, heavy duty. July 1958. (C11366)

B60X gasoline 4-wheel truck, heavy duty. August 1955. (C9047)

B60S gasoline 6-wheel truck. June 1954. (M16206)

B61S diesel 6-wheel truck. June 1959. (C11743)

B61S diesel 6-wheel truck with extra axle.

B61S diesel 6-wheel truck. (424)

B60T gasoline 4-wheel tractor. September 1953. (M15981)

B61T diesel 4-wheel tractor, Mack built integral box sleeper. September 1953. (C7534)

B60T gasoline 4-wheel tractor. April 1954. (M16117)

B60T gasoline 4-wheel tractor. June 1954. (M16203)

84

B60T gasoline 4-wheel tractor. June 1955. (M16447)

B61T with, left-to-right, White, GM, White, GMC, 2 E Model Macks and White trucks.

B61T diesel 4-wheel tractor.

B60T gasoline 4-wheel tractor. March 1956. (M16599R)

B61T (4-wheel) and B61ST (6-wheel) diesel tractors. May 1956. (M16636)

B61T diesel 4-wheel tractor. February 1959. (C11613)

B60T gasoline 4-wheel tractor.

B61T diesel 4-wheel tractor, experimental fiberglass hood. April 1960. (E5095)

B60ST gasoline 6-wheel tractors.

B60ST gasoline 6-wheel tractor. October 1953. (M15994)

B61ST diesel 6-wheel tractor. July 1954. (M16249)

B60ST gasoline 6-wheel tractor. October 1954. (C8206)

B60ST gasoline 6-wheel tractor. November 1954. (M16342)

B61ST diesel 6-wheel tractor. (486)

B60ST gasoline 6-wheel tractor. July 1955. (M16484)

B61ST diesel 6-wheel tractor with cab air-conditioning. October 1956. (C10093)

B62SX gasoline 6-wheel truck, heavy duty. 1961 approximately. (M17510)

B67LT diesel 4-wheel tractor, contoured cab.
December 1957. (C11090)

B65LT diesel 4-wheel tractor, contoured cab. February 1955. (C8464)

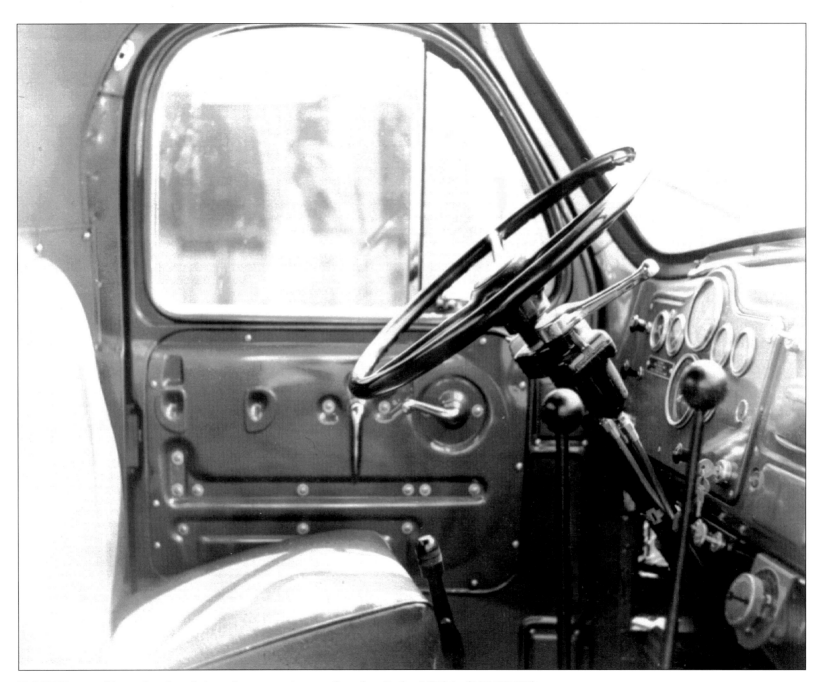

B66LT gasoline 4-wheel tractor, contoured cab. July 1954. (M16225)

B67T diesel 4-wheel tractor. June 1957. (C10859)

B67T diesel 4-wheel tractor. June 1957.
(C10862)

Engine in B67T diesel 4-wheel tractor. June 1957. (C10869)

B67ST diesel 6-wheel tractor. August 1963. (C12623)

B68 gasoline truck and B61 diesel truck of Allied Chemical. (I1654)

B70ST gasoline 6-wheel tractor. May 1955. (M16435)

110

B71S diesel 6-wheel truck. August 1955. (C9080)

B70ST gasoline 6-wheel tractor. October 1956. (C10088)

Engine in B70ST gasoline 6-wheel tractor. October 1956. (C10211)

B73T diesel 4-wheel tractor. April 1958. (C11212)

B753LS turbocharged diesel 6-wheel truck. May 1955. (C8669)

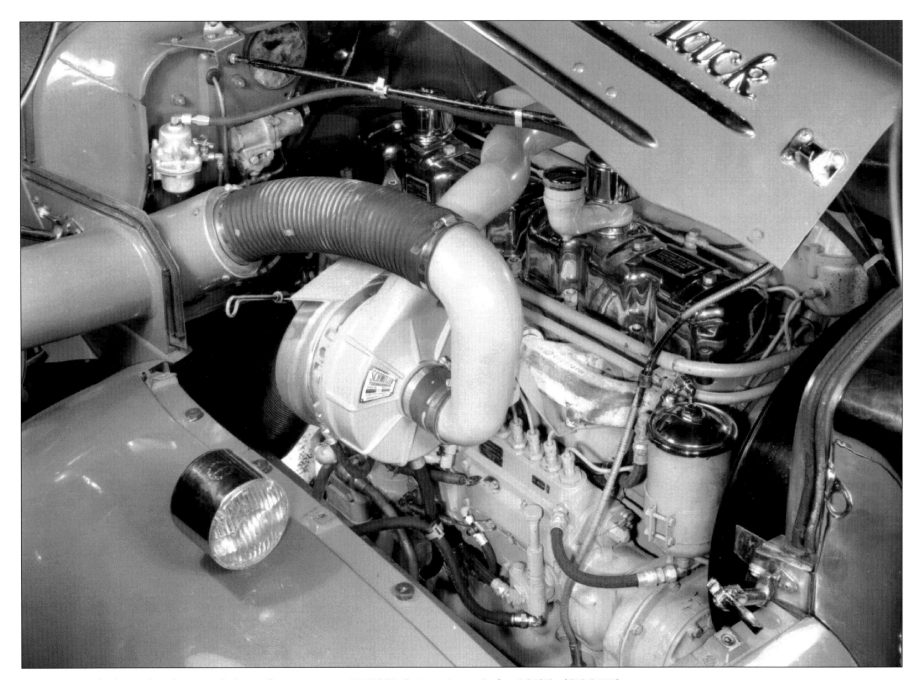

Water cooled turbocharged diesel engine in B753LS tractor. July 1955. (C8977)

B753LST turbocharged diesel 6-wheel tractor. July 1959. (C11761)

B75T diesel 4-wheel tractor. June 1960. (C11979)

Sleeping cab in B75T diesel 4-wheel truck. June 1960. (C11981)

B80 gasoline. (I1561)

B80 gasoline, oil field application.

B80SX gasoline 6-wheel tractor (ID# indicates truck). March 1958. (M17060)

B81 diesel, unloading a generator. (I2112)

B81 diesel.

B80 series, oil field application. (581)

B80 series. (1112)

B813SX turbocharged diesel, 6-wheel truck, heavy duty. (M17470)

B8136SX turbocharged diesel, 6-wheel drive truck, heavy duty. February 1957. (C10505)

B815 diesel V8, 6-wheel tractor.

B815SX diesel V8, 6-wheel truck, heavy duty.

B833SX turbocharged diesel, 6-wheel truck, heavy duty. August 1957. (C10980)

B83SX diesel, 6-wheel truck, heavy duty. March 1956. (C9449)

B85 mock-up. January 1955. (C8431)

B87ST diesel, 6-wheel tractor. (576)

B87ST diesel, 6-wheel tractor. (M17477)

B873SX turbocharged diesel, 6-wheel truck. December 1959. (C11890)

136

B873SX turbocharged diesel, 6-wheel truck. December 1959. (C11891)

Last B model off the line, a B57. April 28, 1966.
(W. M. May, VP Engineering with G. F. Jones, VP
Sales).

B Series Trucks

Model	Years	Units Built	Model	Years	Units Built
B13	1964-65	124	B64	1955-58	119
B20	1953-60	1,113	B65	1955-58	1,623
B23	1963-65	131	B66	1958-65	177
B30	1953-65	4,115	B67	1957-65	8,780
B31	1953-60	177	B68	1960-66	1,503
B33	1955-65	437	B613	1955-66	4,810
B37	1962	1	B615	1962-68	575
B331	1963-64	113	B633	1956-58	486
B332	1963	1	B653	1955-58	93
B334	1963-64	5	B655	1955	10
B41	1953-54	220	B673	1958-65	176
B42	1953-65	19,729	B70	1953-66	1,073
B43	1954-65	1,841	B71	1953-58	522
B44	1955-58	76	B72	1956-65	98
B45	1964-65	142	B73	1955-66	2,520
B46	1958-65	473	B75	1955-66	1,619
B47	1964-65	437	B77	1958-64	113
B421	1954-65	2,144	B79	1961	10
B422	1960-65	923	B733	1955-66	720
B4226	1961-64	14	B753	1955-66	1,825
B424	1961-65	14	B755	1963-66	456
B426	1958-66	221	B773	1957-66	264
B428	1961-62	10	B80	1956-65	368
B462	1960-65	110	B81	1955-66	2,626
B4626	1960	1	B83	1956-66	1,164
B473	1956-62	128	B85	1956-64	77
B50	1953-55	233	B86	1957-59	5
B53	1962-66	2,625	B87	1956-64	75
B57	1964-66	281	B813	1956-66	969
B576	1965-66	26	B815	1963-66	220
B60	1953-63	6,357	B833	1956-66	216
B61	1953-66	47,459	B853	1956-65	29
B62	1954-58	1,463	B873	1956-66	167
B63	1954-58	2,028	B8136	1957-66	85

BIBLIOGRAPHY

Montville, John B., *Mack*, NJ, Walter Haessner, Inc., 1973.

Montville, John B., *Mack, A Living Legend of the Highway*, Tucson, AZ, Aztex Corp., 1979.

Rasmussen, Henry, *Mack, Bulldog of American Highways*, Osceola, WI, Motorbooks International, 1987.

The Iconografix Photo Archive Series includes:

The Iconografix Photo Archive Series is available from direct mail specialty book dealers and bookstores throughout the world, or can be ordered from the publisher.

For information write to:

Iconografix
P.O. Box 609
Osceola, Wisconsin 54020 USA

Telephone: (715) 294-2792
(800) 289-3504 (USA and Canada)
Fax: (715) 294-3414